Famous Explorers

John Cabot

Tanya Larkin

The Rosen Publishing Group's
PowerKids Press™
New York

For Tonino

Published in 2001 by The Rosen Publishing Group, Inc.
29 East 21st Street, New York, NY 10010

Photo Credits: Cover and title page, pp. 11, 15 © SuperStock; pp. 12 © Stock Montage; p. 4, 7, 8, 16, 20 © Granger Collection; p. 22 © FPG International; p. 19 © Bridgeman Art Library; p. 7 © North Wind Pictures; p. 22 Courtesy of Morristown/Morris Township Library.

First Edition

Book Design: Maria E. Melendez and Felicity Erwin

Larkin, Tanya.
    John Cabot/ by Tanya Larkin.
        p. cm.— (Famous explorers)
    Includes index.
    Summary: Describes the life and voyages of the Italian-born explorer who claimed land in the New World for England in 1497.
    ISBN 0-8239-5553-2 (alk. pbk.)
    1. Cabot, John, d. 1498—Juvenile literature. 2. America—Discovery and exploration—English—Juvenile literature. 3. Explorers—America—Biography—Juvenile literature. 4. Explorers—England—Biography—Juvenile literature. 5. Explorers—Italy—Biography—Juvenile literature. [1.Cabot, John, d. 1498. 2. Explorers. 3. America—Discovery and exploration—English.]
    I. Title. II. Series.

E129.C1 L34 2000
970.01'7'092—dc21
[B]   99-048793

Manufactured in the United States of America

Contents

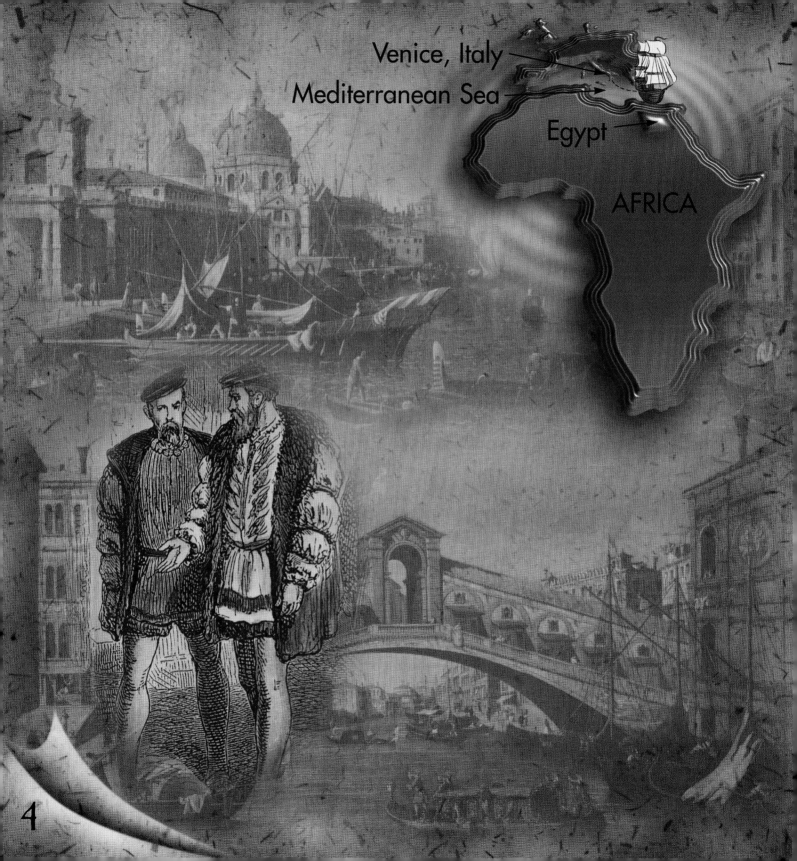

Venice, Italy

Mediterranean Sea

Egypt

AFRICA

4

Born in the Age of Exploration

John Cabot was born in the 1400s in Genoa, Italy, during the Age of Exploration. The Age of Exploration lasted from the 1200s to the 1600s. It was a time in Europe's history when countries were in a race to claim land, riches, and **resources** in the places we now call India, China, and Japan.

John Cabot's family moved to Venice, Italy. Venice was a famous trading **port**. Many explorers sailed from Venice in search of great wealth. When Cabot grew up, he followed in their footsteps. Cabot became a mapmaker and the captain of a trading ship.

Spices were especially valuable in the 1400s because there was no refrigeration. Spices hid the taste of spoiled food. Some people also believed that spices helped fight disease.

John Cabot sailed the Mediterranean Sea bringing Italian goods to Egypt to trade for silk and spices.

The Turks' Taxes

Many of the spices and silks that Cabot brought from Egypt to Europe came from China. **Merchants** carried these goods from China to Egypt in **caravans** across a large desert. People called Turks controlled the land that the merchants passed through. The Turks forced the merchants to pay high **taxes** to pass through their land. This land was known at that time as the Ottoman Empire. Since the merchants who carried the goods paid high taxes, the goods were more expensive for people like Cabot to buy and sell. Cabot wanted to find a sea **route** to China so the merchants would not have to pay the Turks' taxes. This would make the goods they wanted less expensive.

Merchants carried goods along land routes from China to Egypt in caravans.

7.

China

EUROPE

Atlantic
Ocean

AFRICA

Italy

8

John Cabot's New Idea

The ocean Cabot sailed was often called the "Sea of Darkness." Some people believed that it contained dangerous mermaids and sea creatures. Cabot knew that sea travel was rough, but he did not believe these myths.

Cabot was anxious to find a sea route that would make it cheaper for merchants to get to China's riches. He had seen a world map made by the famous Italian mapmaker, Toscanelli. The map showed the vast ocean west of Europe. Like other explorers, Cabot thought that he could sail west across the ocean to reach China, but he had a new idea about how to do this. Cabot knew that the distance around the top or bottom of the globe was much shorter than the distance around the middle. He decided to sail around the top of the globe. He thought that this would make the route to China shorter to **navigate**.

John Cabot used Toscanelli's map of the world to help him find a new way of sailing west to China.

In Search of a King

Explorers in the 1400s needed permission from a king to go on an **expedition**. Some kings even gave explorers money to buy supplies for the voyage. Cabot was excited to try his new route to China, but he had to find a king to support him. He asked the kings of many different countries for help. All of them said no. He did not have any luck until he visited the king of England, King Henry VII, in 1496. Cabot told King Henry VII that his sea route would make it cheaper for English merchants to trade with China. King Henry VII gave Cabot permission to make the trip.

When he was born in Italy, John Cabot was named Giovanni Caboto. In Italian, Cabot's last name, Caboto, means "coasting vessel." When he sailed for England, he changed his name to its English version, John Cabot.

This is a picture of King Henry VII of England and a map of China.

CHINA

NEWFOUNDLAND

IRELAND

ENGLAND

The Matthew

On May 2, 1497, Cabot set out on an old ship called the *Matthew* to find the sea route to China. It was filled with mice, roaches, and rats. The *Matthew* had once been used to trade fish, tar, and wool, so it smelled of all these things. Cabot sailed from England around the southern tip of Ireland. During the voyage west, Cabot's crew slept and ate on deck. They ate fish, salted beef, and biscuits. Drinking salty sea water is dangerous because the salt can make you sick. Cabot and his crew brought fresh water from home. During a storm, they sometimes caught rain in the sails of the ship and kept it to drink later.

The *Matthew* was a special ship. It had decks at the front and back. Most ships just had a hull, or a large wooden body without decks. Water on the hull often stayed in the bottom of the boat, but the decks on the *Matthew* helped keep the ship drier.

John Cabot and his crew on the deck of the Matthew, *off the coast of Newfoundland in 1497.*

Two Flags and a Cross

Cabot and his crew stepped foot on land on June 24, 1497, two months after they set sail. Cabot planted a cross and the English flag into the rocky ground. These symbols showed that he claimed the island for the church and for England. Cabot was proud of his homeland, Venice, even though he was sailing for England's king, so he left the flag of Venice, too. Cabot thought that he had discovered an island off the coast of China. Really, he was on an island near the land that we now call Canada. No one knows for sure exactly where Cabot landed, but he is known as the first explorer to reach North America for the English.

John Cabot claiming an island in the name of King Henry VII of England, in 1497.

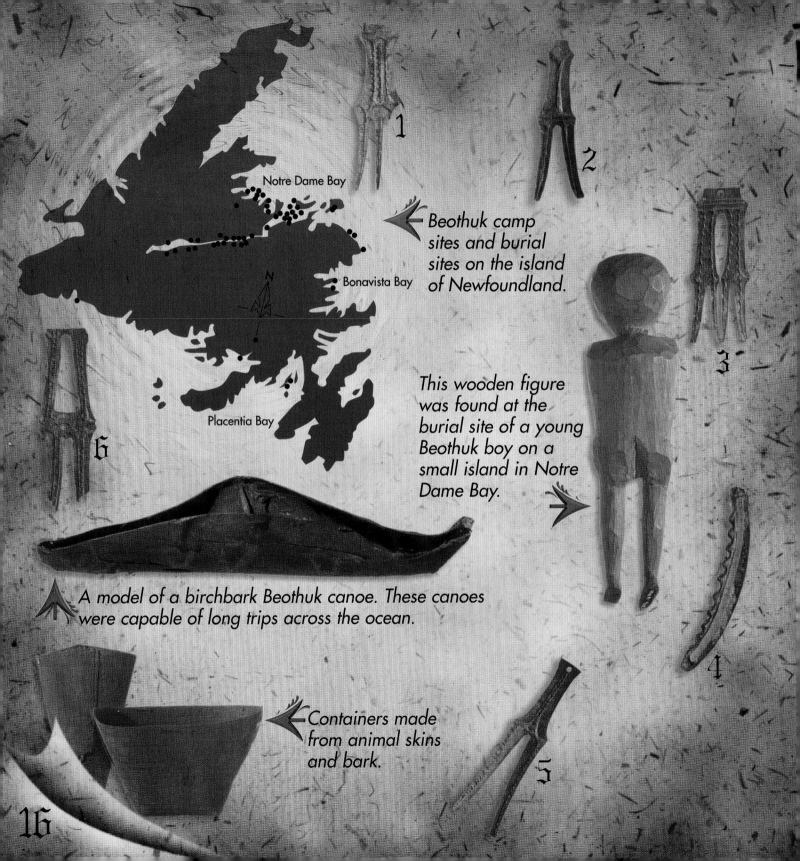

1

2

3

Notre Dame Bay

Beothuk camp sites and burial sites on the island of Newfoundland.

Bonavista Bay

This wooden figure was found at the burial site of a young Beothuk boy on a small island in Notre Dame Bay.

6

Placentia Bay

4

A model of a birchbark Beothuk canoe. These canoes were capable of long trips across the ocean.

Containers made from animal skins and bark.

5

16

The Beothuk People

Cabot landed on an island off the coast of Newfoundland. This is where a group of people called the Beothuks were living. The Beothuks lived off the land by hunting or finding food like berries and nuts. When Cabot landed, the Beothuks probably had moved inland to find food. Cabot and his men did not meet any of the Beothuks. They did find traps that the Beothuks used to catch animals and a needle that they used to make fishing nets. Cabot and his sailors were disappointed that they had not found silk and spices. There were lots of fish in this area, though, and Cabot and his crew caught many to dry and store for food.

The Beothuks smeared red ocher on their faces and bodies as part of their religion. Ocher is a type of soil dug out of the ground. This is why the Europeans named the Native Americans "Red Indians."

Numbers 1 through 6 are bone pendants found at a burial site. They were attached to skin burial bags or hung on clothing. Some of the sites on this map are 1,300 years old.

The Search for the Northwest Passage

After landing on the island, Cabot continued to sail south hoping to reach China. Cabot was determined to find a sea route through this land that would lead to the **continent** of China. This **waterway** that Cabot hoped to find would later be called the Northwest Passage. Many explorers after Cabot would seek this sea route through North America that connects the Atlantic and Pacific oceans.

When he reached what is today called the Saint Lawrence River, Cabot thought he had found the passage. He wanted to keep sailing, but the expedition started running out of food. Cabot ordered the *Matthew* to sail back to England.

Explorers, like Cabot, searched for ways to get to China to find silk and other riches.